How to Solve Problems
the Easy way

A Step by Step Guide to Improving Your Problem Solving Skills

By Meir Liraz

(Including 10 Special Bonuses)

Published by Liraz Publishing

www.BizMove.com

Table of Contents

1. Introduction

As the owner of your own business you deal with problems on an almost daily basis. Being familiar with effective Problem Solving Techniques can dramatically affect the growth of your business.

Although you find solutions to your problems, many businessmen and women are not really skilled in the methods of problem solving, and when solutions fail, they fault themselves for misjudgment. The problem is typically not misjudgment but rather a lack of skill.

This guide instructs you in some problem solving techniques. Crucial to the success of a business faced with problems is your understanding of just what the problems are, defining them, finding solutions, and selecting the best solutions for the situations. This guide explains the following.

How to identify a problem. How to respond to it. The different techniques and methods used in problem-solving. How to find alternative solutions. How to select the best solution for the situation. Designing a Plan of Action. How to implement the Plan of Action. How to assess the success of the solution and the Plan of Action.

Introduction to Problem Solving Techniques

What is a problem. A problem is a situation that presents difficulty or perplexity. Problems come in many shapes and sizes. For example, it can be:

Something did not work as it should and you don't know how or why. Something you need is unavailable, and something must be found to take its place. Employees are undermining a new program. The market is not buying. What do you do to survive? Customers are complaining. How do you handle their complaints?

Where do problems come from? Problems arise from every facet of human and mechanical functions as well as from nature. Some problems we cause ourselves (e.g., a hasty choice was made and the wrong person was selected for the job); other problems are caused by forces beyond our control (e.g., a warehouse is struck by lightning and burns down).

Problems are a natural, everyday occurrence of life, and in order to suffer less from the tensions and frustrations they cause, we must learn how to deal with them in a rational, logical fashion.

If we accept the fact that problems will arise on a regular basis, for a variety of reasons, and from a variety of sources, we can:

learn to approach problems from an objective point of view; learn how to anticipate some of them; and prevent some of them from becoming larger problems.

To accomplish this, you need to learn the process of problem solving.

Here, we will instruct you in the basic methods of problem-solving. It is a step by step guide which you can easily follow and practice. As you follow this guide, you will eventually develop some strategies of your own that work in concert with the problem-solving process described in this guide.

Keep in mind, though, as you read that this is not a comprehensive analysis of the art of problem-solving but rather a practical, systematic, and simplified, yet effective, way to approach problems considering the limited time and information most business owners and managers have. In addition, some problems are so complex that they require the additional help of experts in the field, so be prepared to accept the fact that some problems are beyond one person's ability, skill, and desire to succeed.

2. Identifying the Problem

Before a problem can be solved, you must first recognize that a problem exists. Here is where your approach to problem-solving is crucial. You should not allow the problem to intimidate you. You should approach it rationally and remind yourself that every problem is solvable if it is tackled appropriately.

Fear can block your ability to think clearly, but if you:

1. Follow a workable procedure for finding solutions;

2. Accept the fact that you can't foresee everything;

3. Assume that the solution you select is your best option at the time; and

4. Accept the possibility that things may change and your solution fail;

you will then enter the problem-solving process rationally, You should try to view it as an intellectual exercise. Once you recognize that a problem exists, your next step is to identify the problem. First, you need to discover how the problem occurred. Ask yourself the following questions:

1. Did something go wrong?

2. Did something breakdown?

3. Were there unexpected results or outcome?

4. Is something that once worked no longer working?

Second, you need to know the nature of the problem:

1. Is it people, operational, technical, etc.?

2. Is it with a particular department, product or service, etc.?

3. Is it something tangible or intangible?

4. Is it an external or internal problem?

Third, you need to decide how significant the problem is. Based on the level of significance, you may choose to deal with the problem or not to deal with it. Sometimes what you think is a small problem, when analyzed, proves to be a major problem. The reverse is also true. To determine this, you should ask yourself the following types of questions:

1. Is it disrupting operations?

2. Is it hampering sales?

3. Is it causing conflict among people?

4. Is it an everyday occurrence or is it infrequent?

5. Is it affecting personnel and their productivity?

6. Is it common or unusual?

7. Is it affecting goals, and if yes, which ones?

8. Is it affecting customers, vendors, and any other external people?

Fourth, you should narrow down the type of problem:

1. Is it basically a problem which occurred in the past and the main concern is to make certain that it doesn't occur again?

2. Is it a problem which currently exists and the main concern is to clear up the situation?

3. Is it a problem which might occur in the future and the basic concern is planning and taking action before the problem arises?

The answer to all of the above questions will help you focus on the true problem. You cannot effectively research the causes of a problem until you have a clear understanding of what the problem is. Sometimes, people spend many hours on what they perceive as a problem only to find out, after seeking the causes, that something else was really the problem.

In order to appropriately identify the problem and its causes, you must do some research. To do this, simply list all the previous questions in checklist form, and keeping the checklist handy, go about gathering as much information as you possibly can. Keep in mind the relative importance and urgency of the problem, as well as your own time limitations. Then interview the people involved with the problem, asking them the questions on your checklist.

After you've gathered the information and reviewed it, you will have a pretty clear understanding of the problem and what the major causes of the problem are. At this point, you can research the causes further through observation and additional interviewing. Now, you should summarize the problem as briefly as possible, list all the causes you have identified, and list all the areas the problem seems to be affecting.

Before proceeding to finding solutions, there is some additional research that could be done. If possible and if warranted, you might wish to find out:

1. What has previously been done in regards to this problem.

2. What have other companies done.

3. What formal knowledge might you need to acquire.

4. What has been learned from past experience.

5. What do experts say about the problem.

3. Roadblocks to Problem Solving

Many of us serve as our own roadblocks in solving problems. There are a variety of roadblocks to watch for in order to effectively use the technique of problem solving:

1. Watch out for old habits.

2. Check your perceptions.

3. Overcome your fears.

4. Be careful of assumptions.

5. Don't be tied to a problem; try to look at it with detachment.

6. Don't let yourself procrastinate.

7. Control your inclination for reactive solutions.

8. Control your inclination for rash solutions.

9. Avoid emotional responses and always attempt to be rational.

10. Be aware that the nature of a problem can change.

11. Do not skip steps in the problem solving process.

At this point, you are ready to check your understanding of the problem. You've already identified the problem, broken it all down into all its facets, narrowed it down, done research on it, and you are avoiding typical roadblocks. On a large pad, write down the problem, including all of the factors, the areas it affects, and what the effects are. For a better visual understanding, you may also wish to diagram the problem showing cause and effect.

Study what you have written down and/or diagrammed. Call in your employees and discuss your analysis with them. Based on their feedback, you may decide to revise. Once you think you fully understand the causes and effects of the problem, summarize the problem as succinctly and as simply as possible.

4. How to Find Solutions

There are a number of methods for finding solutions. We will describe five thinking methods below, but we recommend that you use a number of them in finding solutions. The first four methods described are unconventional and more innovative. They allow you the possibility of arriving at a novel solution. The fifth method is a more typical and straightforward method.

1. Association: There are three types of associative thinking. This type of thinking is basically a linking process either through similarity, difference, or contiguity. For example, contiguity finds solutions from things that are connected through proximity, sequence, and cause and effect. The process works as follows: List as many parts of the problem you can think of. Then giving yourself a short time limit, list as many words or ideas that have either proximity, sequence, or related cause and effect to the ones you have listed. For example, a contiguous association might be "misplaced work - cluttered desk" (proximity); "misplaced work - rushing" (sequence); "misplaced work - irate customer" (cause and effect).

Associative thinking taps the resources of the mind. It brings into focus options you might not have considered if you stuck to ideas only directly related to the problem. As a result of associative thinking, you might find other relationships embedded in the problem that will lead to a better solution.

2. Analogy: This thinking method is a way of finding solutions through comparisons. The process is based on comparing the different facets of the problem with other problems that may or may not have similar facets. An analogy might go like this: "Employees have been coming in late to work quite often; how can I get them to be at work on time? This to me is like soldiers being late for a battle. Would soldiers come late to a battle? Why not?" By, comparing the situation of workers to the situation of soldiers, you may find a solution for a way to motivate employees to come to work on time.

3. Brainstorming: This thinking method is based on a free, non-threatening, anything goes atmosphere. You can brainstorm alone or with a group of people. Most often a group of people from diverse backgrounds is preferable. The process works like this: The problem is explained to the group and each member is encouraged to throw out as many ideas for solutions as he or she can think of no matter how ridiculous or far-fetched they may sound. All the ideas are discussed among the group, revised, tossed out, expanded, etc. based on the group's analysis of them. Based on the group's grasp of the effectiveness of each idea, the best ones are selected for closer review. For example, the group of people might throw out for consideration any thoughts they might have on how to increase sales or improve profits.

4. Intuition: This mode of thinking is based on hunches. It is not, as some think, irrational. Intuition or hunches are built on a strong foundation of facts and experiences that are buried somewhere in the subconscious. All the things you know and have experienced can lead you to believe that something might be true although you've never actually experienced that reality. Use your intuition as much as possible but check it against the reality of the situation.

5. Analytical Thinking: This thinking method is based on analysis. It is the most conventional and logical of all the methods and follows a step by step pattern.

a. Examine each cause of the problem. Then for each cause, based on your direct knowledge and experience, list the solutions that logically would seem to solve the problem.

b. Check the possible solutions you arrive at with the research you have compiled on how the problem was solved by others.

Using each thinking technique, search for solutions.
Keep a running list of all of them, even the ones
that seem far out, too simple, or even impossible.
The effect of this is to give you a rich pool of ideas
that will lead you to the best solution.

5. Sorting Out the Best Solution

Go through your long list of solutions and cross-out those that obviously won't work. Those ideas are not wasted for they impact on those ideas that remain. In other words, the best ideas you select may be revised based on the ideas that wouldn't work. With the remaining solutions, use what is called the "Force Field Analysis Technique." This is basically an analysis technique which breaks the solution down into its positive effects and negative effects. To do this, write each solution you are considering on a separate piece of paper. Below the solution, draw a line vertically down the center of the paper. Label one column advantages and one column disadvantages.

Now, some more analytical thinking comes into play. Analyzing each facet of the solution and its effect on the problem, listing each of the advantages and disadvantages you can think of.

One way to help you think of the advantages and disadvantages is to role-play each solution. Call in a few of your employees and play out each solution. Ask them for their reactions. Based on what you observe and on their feedback, you will have a better idea of the advantages and disadvantages of each solution you are considering.

After you complete this process for each solution, select those solutions which have the most advantages. At this point, you should be considering only two or three. In order to select the most appropriate solution, you should check each solution against the following criteria:

Cost effectiveness; Time constraints; Availability of manpower, material, etc.; Your own intuition.

Before you actually implement the solution, you should evaluate it. Ask yourself these questions:

1. Are the objectives of the solution sound and clear and not complex?

2. Will the solution achieve the objectives?

3. What are the possibilities it will fail and in what way?

6. The Plan of Action

Finding the solution does not mean the problem is solved. Now, you need to design a plan of action so that the solution gets carried out properly. Designing and carrying out the plan of action is equally as important as the solution. The best solution can fail because it is not implemented correctly. When designing the plan of action, consider the following:

Who will be involved in the solution; Who will be affected by the solution; What course of action will be taken; How should the course of action be presented to company employees, customers, vendors, etc.; When will it happen - the time frame; Where will it happen; How will it happen; What is needed to make it happen.

Design a plan of action chart including all the details you need to consider to carry it out and when each phase should happen. Keep in mind, though, that the best plans have setbacks for any number of reasons - from a key person being out for illness to a supplier shipping material late. So remember that your dates are only target dates. Solutions and plans of action must be flexible. Expect some things to be revised.

7. Evaluating the Plan of Action

Before you implement the plan of action, you should analyze it to see if you've considered as many of the variables as possible. Some questions you might ask yourself are:

1. Is there adequate staff to carry it out?

2. Is the plan detailed yet simple enough for those affected to know what to expect and how to carry it out?

3. Will it embarrass anyone - manager, employee, customer, vendor, etc.?

4. Is the time frame realistic and feasible?

5. Are there special conditions which may have been overlooked?

6. Who should be informed?

7. Who should be involved?

8. Who should be responsible for each aspect and/or phase?

9. Is the plan of action cost effective?

10. Does the plan have a public relations component?

8. Obstacles You May Encounter

There are a number of obstacles you may encounter when you implement your plan of action. It is, therefore, advisable that you devise ways to overcome them. Try not to allow obstacles to prevent you from reaching your goals. Some obstacles to watch for are:

1. Not receiving material and/or equipment on time;

2. Other situations which might arise and deflect your attention from this problem;

3. Procrastination;

4. A power struggle among managers and/or employees;

5. Resistance to change - a natural human condition.

Resistance to change and company-wide acceptance is typically the biggest obstacle. The best way to overcome them is to build a public relations component into your plan of action. The key question to ask yourself is, "How will I get my people to support the solution and make it work?" Some effective methods for accomplishing this are:

1. Have as many managers and employees involved in the problem solving process as possible.

2. Advertise the problem and solution to your employees through memos, newsletters, and posters, showing the advantages and disadvantages of the solution but proving it is better than the conditions which currently exist.

3. Establish a schedule of meetings where different groups of employees can be exposed to the solution and ask them for their feedback.

4. If necessary, develop a training program so that managers and employees feel competent in carrying out the solution.

5. Involve key leaders who wield impact and influence others.

The key to a successful PR campaign is involving, as much as possible, the people who are affected by the problem. The benefits of doing so is that they will understand the problem better and why the solution is an effective one. The result will be that they will be more likely to not only support your solution but also make sure that it works. Many times the solutions we select for problems don't work because employees sabotage them, not because they are not inherently good solutions. Employees may resist change, especially if they feel threatened. Involving employees will assuage their fears.

9. Simulating the Solution / Plan of Action

Before you implement the plan of action on a full scale, you should select a small group of managers and employees and role play the solution in the work setting. Observe the group as they carry out the solution and take note of:

1. How they carry out the solution;

2. Their reactions to the solution;

3. Their understanding of the solution;

4. The effectiveness of the tools they are using in carrying out the solution;

5. Their resistance to change and reverting back to the previous behaviors.

Based on what you observe, you may need to revise some of your plans.

10. Successful Implementation

To assure the successful implementation successful implementation of your solution and plan of action, remember the following:

1. Prepare your staff well in advance;

2. Train your staff well in advance;

3. Order equipment, material, etc., well in advance;

4. If necessary, hire new staff and do so well in advance;

5. Use PR at every meeting and in memos as much as possible;

6. Evaluate the effects of each phase as it is implemented and make the necessary adjustments;

7. Attempt to remain flexible and open-minded.

Evaluating the Success of Your Solution

As each phase of your plan of action is implemented, you should ask yourself whether your goals were achieved, how well they were achieved, and did it work smoothly. To check your own perceptions of the results, get as much feedback as possible from your managers and from your employees. What you may think is working may not be working well in the eyes of your people. Always remember that they are one of your most valuable tools in successfully carrying out your solution.

11. How to handle stress

You need stress in your life! Does that surprise you? Perhaps so, but it is quite true. Without stress, life would be dull and unexciting. Stress adds flavor, challenge, and opportunity to life. Too much stress, however, can seriously affect your physical and mental well-being. A major challenge in this stress-filled world of today is to make the stress in your life work for you instead of against you.

Stress is with us all the time. It comes from mental or emotional activity and physical activity. It is unique and personal to each of us. So personal, in fact, that what may be relaxing to one person may be stressful to another. For example, if you're a busy executive who likes to keep busy all the time, "taking it easy" at the beach on a beautiful day may feel extremely frustrating, nonproductive, and upsetting. You may be emotionally distressed from "doing nothing."

Too much emotional stress can cause physical illness such as high blood pressure, ulcers, or even heart disease; physical stress from work or exercise is not likely to cause such ailments. The truth is that physical exercise can help you to relax and to handle

MEIR LIRAZ

your mental or emotional stress.

Hans Selye, M.D., a recognized expert in the field, has defined stress as a "non-specific response of the body to a demand." The important issue is learning how our bodies respond to these demands. When stress becomes prolonged or particularly frustrating, it can become harmful-causing distress or "bad stress." Recognizing the early signs of distress and then doing something about them can make an important difference in the quality of your life, and may actually influence your survival.

Reacting to Stress

To use stress in a positive way and prevent it from becoming distress, you should become aware of your own reactions to stressful events. The body responds to stress by going through three stages: (1) alarm, (2) resistance, and (3) exhaustion.

Let's take the example of a typical commuter in rush-hour traffic. If a car suddenly pulls out in front of him, his initial alarm reaction may include fear of an accident, anger at the driver who committed the action, and general frustration. His body may respond in the alarm stage by releasing hormones into the bloodstream which cause his face to flush, perspiration to form, his stomach to have a sinking feeling, and his arms and legs to tighten. The next stage is resistance, in which the body repairs damage caused by the stress. If the stress of driving continues with repeated close calls or traffic jams, however, his body will not have time to make repairs. He may become so conditioned to expect potential problems when he drives that he tightens up at the beginning of each commuting day. Eventually, he may even develop one of the diseases of stress, such as migraine headaches, high blood pressure, backaches, or insomnia. While it is impossible to live completely free of stress and distress, it is possible to prevent some distress as well as to minimize its impact when it can't be avoided.

Helping Yourself

When stress does occur, it is important to recognize and deal with it. Here are some suggestions for ways to handle stress. As you begin to understand more about how stress affects you as an individual, you will come up with your own ideas of helping to ease the tensions.

Try physical activity. When you are nervous, angry, or upset, release the pressure through exercise or physical activity. Running, walking, playing tennis, or working in your garden are just some of the activities you might try. Physical exercise will relieve that "up tight" feeling, relax you, and turn the frowns into smiles. Remember, your body and your mind work together.

Share your stress. It helps to talk to someone about your concerns and worries. Perhaps a friend, family member, teacher, or counselor can help you see your problem in a different light. If you feel your problem is serious, you might seek professional help from a psychologist, psychiatrist, or social worker. Knowing when to ask for help may avoid more serious problems later.

Know your limits. If a problem is beyond your

control and cannot be changed at the moment, don't fight the situation. Learn to accept what is-for now-until such time when you can change it.

Take care of yourself. You are special. Get enough rest and eat well. If you are irritable and tense from lack of sleep or if you are not eating correctly, you will have less ability to deal with stressful situations. If stress repeatedly keeps you from sleeping, you should ask your doctor for help.

Make time for fun. Schedule time for both work and recreation. Play can be just as important to your well-being as work; you need a break from your daily routine to just relax and have fun.

Be a participant. One way to keep from getting bored, sad, and lonely is to go where it's all happening: Sitting alone can make you feel frustrated. Instead of feeling sorry for yourself, get involved and become a participant. Offer your services in neighborhood or volunteer organizations. Help yourself by helping other people. Get involved in the world and the people around you, and you'll find they will be attracted to you. You're on your way to making new friends and enjoying new activities.

Check off your tasks. Trying to take care of everything at once can seem overwhelming, and, as a result, you may not accomplish anything, Instead, make a list of what tasks you have to do, then do one at a time, checking them off as they're completed. Give priority to the most important ones and do those first.

Must you always be right? Do other people upset you - particularly when they don't do things your way? Try cooperation instead of confrontation; it's better than fighting and always being "right:" A little give and take on both sides will reduce the strain and make you both feel more comfortable.

It's OK to cry. A good cry can be a healthy way to bring relief to your anxiety, and it might even prevent a headache or other physical consequence. Take some deep breaths; they also release tension.

Create a quiet scene. You can't always run away, but you can "dream the impossible dream." A quiet country scene painted mentally, or on canvas, can take you out of the turmoil of a stressful situation. Change the scene by reading a good book or playing beautiful music to create a sense of peace and tranquillity.

Avoid self-medication. Although you can use drugs to relieve stress temporarily, drugs do not remove the conditions that caused the stress in the first place. Drugs, in fact, may be habit-forming and create more stress than they take away. They should be taken :only on the advice of your doctor.

4. The Art of Relaxation

The best strategy for avoiding stress is to learn how to relax. Unfortunately, many people try to relax at the same pace that they lead the rest of their lives. For a while, tune out your worries about time, productivity, and "doing right." You will find satisfaction in just being, without striving. Find activities that give you pleasure and that are good for your mental and physical well-being. Forget about always winning. Focus on relaxation, enjoyment, and health. Be good to yourself.

How to Overcome Fear and Anxiety

When faced with fear, we often talk ourselves out of taking action. Most of the time, we have nothing to lose and everything to gain!

1. Breathe!

When we are excited, we get body sensations that can stop us. Stop, take some deep breaths and then proceed. This is especially important to help your voice sound calm when your knees are shaking.

2. Remember, it isn't about you!

When you get rejection, it is usually because the other person doesn't need what you are offering. It isn't personal. They may just be having a bad day. Or if they are genuinely a nasty person, they gave you a break by not prolonging the relationship!

3. Picture The WORST

Can you live through that? We awfulize most things and imagine the outcome far worse than it usually is. Ask yourself, what is the worst that can happen? Most of the time, you can handle it!

4. **Master The Topic**

If we feel confident in our knowledge, the fear about sharing it with others decreases. Even if they don't see value or agree with us, we feel okay, because we have developed an expertise that gives us confidence in ourselves.

5. **Put something at stake or give yourself reward**

A reward or penalty that is big enough will motivate sometimes. A sales trainer coached a real estate agent in making regular prospecting calls to write a check for $1000 to his ex-wife and have his secretary send it any day he did not make the number of prospecting calls he said he would.

6. **Get a Buddy**

Taking on something fearful with another person often will get you through it and keep you from having those dialogues in your head that try to talk you out of it. A coach can also help shine light into those dark areas!

7. **Talk about it out loud**

Once you identify the fear and talk about it out

loud, it will often diminish. Another technique is to close your eyes and picture yourself doing that thing you are afraid to do. Now run through the same scene but do it very fast. Now run through it very slow, next make it silly, make it brighter, make it dimmer. Has some of the fear dissipated?

8. Read something inspirational or listen to tapes.

Play your favorite motivational tape or read something inspirational right before you take action to help your mind focus on what is POSSIBLE rather than what could derail you. Think about how you will feel when you have taken action. Write down the top 10 feelings you'll have when you have done this thing!

9. Use your strengths-take the easy way!

Sometimes we focus on thinking we "should" do things that just aren't our strengths. Take a look to see if you can accomplish what you want some other way. What easy ones can you do first? How can you leverage what you already have without having to tackle an unknown.

10. If you have a frog to swallow, do it quickly

Don't look at it too long. Sometimes, there is no way around the fact, you are going to have to take an action that is fearful. The longer you fret about it, there more energy you waste. JUST DO IT!!!!

How to Be Empowered

Contrary to common belief, the most effective control over one's life can be gained in an almost effortless manner. The truly empowered person "has it together", exudes a glowing poise that is apparent to others. Here are ten steps whereby you can begin experience empowerment in your own life.

1. Start from where you are and take one step at a time.

When you think about it, that's the only place you CAN start, i.e., where you are at this moment. Begin with your present perceptions, understandings, and strengths and move forward, one step at a time. In this world of objectives, goals and big plans, we often focus too much on the future with the result that our ability to concentrate fully on the present is severely compromised. Yet, it is only in the present that we can make a difference.

2. Examine your resistance points--the things that irritate you, limit you, or cause you to react.

We often resist what we most need to learn. The

next time you find yourself resisting new information, a particular situation, or something someone else is saying, ask yourself: What is it that is really bothering me about this? Is there something that I need to learn?

3. Recognize that whatever you are experiencing at this very moment is appropriate to your need to grow.

Implicit in this "rule of appropriateness" is the concept that there is a larger plan of which you are an integral part. Until you're willing to acknowledge the possibility that such a plan exists, you will never be able to see it!

4. Stop worrying about whether others are getting theirs!

It's easy to become preoccupied about what the other person is doing, getting, achieving, etc. This kind of worrying is useless and wastes time and energies that are better spent on yourself.

5. Realize that it doesn't matter what happened to you or who did it to you; the only thing that matters is what you do about it.

What happened and who did it to you are in the

past. You can't change the past, you can only change your perception of it. The ONLY thing that counts is what you do NOW in order to move forward.

6. **Learn to withhold judgment.**

To withhold judgment is to accept what is. How often in conversation do you find yourself mentally correcting, criticizing, or re-phrasing? when you do, you risk missing the real message which may not be in the words themselves. Rather than saying to yourself, "that's inaccurate" or "he/she is wrong", try accepting the statement as simply a representation of the way that person thinks, feels or what he/she intends to convey. This simple technique can open up a whole realm of hidden meaning, AND it enables you to respond more objectively and dispassionately.

7. **Learn to operate holistically by opening up to the other possibilities that are always there.**

There is always more than one way to solve a problem. You're most likely to get "stuck" when you foreclose your options by setting up conditions, demands, expectations, fears, positions and prejudices.

8. Complete your unfinished business.

Most of us have "unfinished business"--failures, a relationship gone sour, or a good deed left undone. Getting beyond ("completing") is not always easy, but there's a three-step process that, if followed, can do wonders for your psyche. It's this: (1) Acknowledge the wrong, mistake, screw-up, etc. to yourself, (2) Admit it to one other person, preferably the person you've wronged and, in the latter case, apologize and ask simply: "What can I do to make this right with you?" (Sometimes there really isn't much you can do, but the simple act of asking is healing in itself), and (3) Move ON. You've admitted your mistake, taken whatever corrective action you could, and now it's time to go forward. This third step takes discipline, but it works.

9. When faced with an apparently hopeless situation, take action, any action.

There's something called the "logjam" theory that applies here: when logs in a stream become all jammed up, moving ANY ONE log frees the others to move, because the act of moving a single piece creates space which in turn allows the other pieces to move. It's important to recognize that you're not trying to reach a final solution in a single move; you're simply taking "one step at a time" (Step#1)

10. Consider the wisdom of doing absolutely nothing!

As with the rule of appropriateness (above), there's a hidden assumption here, namely, that we each possess an inner wisdom that is always available if we know how to tap into it. Call it intuition, spiritual sense, whatever, the fact is that this "still small voice" is audible only when we are very quiet. It's a bit like a point in which you can see the bottom only when the surface is calm and the water nu-muddied. Doing nothing means exactly that: nothing physically, nothing mentally, nothing at all! The Japanese call it, "kokoro-no-mizu", literally, a "mind as water"--smooth, flowing and undisturbed. Try it. It works, and it's fun!

Appendix: Special Free Bonuses

You can access your free bonuses here:

https://www.bizmove.com/bizgifts.htm

Here's what you get:

#1 How to Be a Good Manager and Leader; 120 Tips to improve your Leadership Skills (Leadership Video Guide).

Learn how to improve your leadership skills and become a better manager and leader. Here's how to be the boss people want to give 200 percent for. In this video you'll discover 120 powerful tips and strategies to motivate and inspire your people to bring out the best in them.

#2 Small Business Management: Essential Ingredients for Success (eBook Guide)

Discover scores of business management tricks, secrets and shortcuts. This Ebook guide does far more than impart knowledge - it inspires action.

#3 How to Manage Yourself for Success; 90 Tips to Better Manage Yourself and Your Time (Self Management Video Guide)

You are responsible for everything that happens in your life. Learn to accept total responsibility for yourself. If you don't manage yourself, then you are letting others have control of your life. In this video you'll discover 90 powerful tips and strategies to better manage yourself for success.

#4 80 Best Inspirational Quotes for Success (Motivational Video Guide)

For this video we scanned thousands of motivational and inspirational quotes to bring you this collection of the best 80 motivational quotes for success in life.

#5 Top 10 Habits to Adopt From Highly Successful People (Self Growth Video Guide)

In this video you'll discover the top 10 habits of highly successful people that you can adopt and achieve success in your life.

#6 Personal Branding: How to Make a Killer First Impression (Self Promotion Video Guide)

This video deals with personal branding. While promoting your personal brand, you'll discover in this video the ten most effective things you can do to make the best first impression possible.

#7 How to Advance Your Career 10 Times Faster (Career Advancement Video Guide)

The most important thing to remember about your

career today is that you need to be responsible for your own future. In this video you'll discover 10 powerful strategies to advance your career faster.

#8 How to Get Success in Life; 10 Strategies to Attract the Life You Want (Self Actualization Video Guide)

To have more, we must be more of who we are. The secret is in the doing; none of it matters until we do something about it. In this video you'll discover 10 powerful strategies to attract the life you want.

#9 A Comprehensive Package of Business Tools

Here's a collection featuring dozens of business related templates, worksheets, forms, and plans; covering finance, starting a business, marketing, business planning, sales, and general management.

#10 People Management Skills: How to Deal with Difficult Employees (Managing People Video Guide)

Problem behavior on the part of employees can erupt for a variety of reasons. In this video you'll discover the top ten ideas for dealing with difficult employees.

* * * *

www.ingramcontent.com/pod-product-compliance
Lightning Source LLC
Chambersburg PA
CBHW070839220526
45466CB00002B/823